This notebook belongs to:

_____

Published by: Character Designs

PROJECT NAME: _____   NOTE: _____

Customer-Journey Map				Date :
Persona	User State	Journey (inc. tasks)	Channels	Content

stomer-Journey Map				Date:
sona	User State	Journey (inc. tasks)	Channels	Content

PROJECT NAME: _____   NOTE: _____

Customer-Journey Map				Date:
Persona	User State	Journey (inc. tasks)	Channels	Content

ECT NAME: _____   NOTE: _____

sona	User State	Journey (inc. tasks)	Channels	Content

stomer-Journey Map   Date :

Customer-Journey Map

Date :

Persona	User State	Journey (inc. tasks)	Channels	Content

stomer-Journey Map				Date :
sona	User State	Journey (inc. tasks)	Channels	Content

PROJECT NAME: _____   NOTE: _____

Customer-Journey Map				Date:
Persona	User State	Journey (inc. tasks)	Channels	Content

stomer-Journey Map				Date:
sona	User State	Journey (inc. tasks)	Channels	Content

PROJECT NAME: _____   NOTE: _____

Customer-Journey Map				Date :
Persona	User State	Journey (inc. tasks)	Channels	Content

stomer-Journey Map				Date :
sona	User State	Journey (inc. tasks)	Channels	Content

Customer-Journey Map   Date :

Persona	User State	Journey (inc. tasks)	Channels	Content

slomer-Journey Map				Date :
sona	User State	Journey (inc. tasks)	Channels	Content

PROJECT NAME: _____   NOTE: _____

Customer-Journey Map

Date:

Persona	User State	Journey (inc. tasks)	Channels	Content

JECT NAME: _____   NOTE: _____

stomer-Journey Map				Date:
sona	User State	Journey (inc. tasks)	Channels	Content

PROJECT NAME: _____   NOTE: _____

Customer-Journey Map				Date:
Persona	User State	Journey (inc. tasks)	Channels	Content

stomer-Journey Map   Date:

sona	User State	Journey (inc. tasks)	Channels	Content

PROJECT NAME: _____   NOTE: _____

Customer-Journey Map				Date:
Persona	User State	Journey (inc. tasks)	Channels	Content

stomer-Journey Map				Date :
sona	User State	Journey (inc. tasks)	Channels	Content

PROJECT NAME: _____   NOTE: _____

Customer-Journey Map				Date:
Persona	User State	Journey (inc. tasks)	Channels	Content

slomer-Journey Map				Date:
sona	User State	Journey (inc. tasks)	Channels	Content

Customer-Journey Map

Date :

Persona	User State	Journey (inc. tasks)	Channels	Content

stomer-Journey Map   Date :

sona	User State	Journey (inc. tasks)	Channels	Content

Customer-Journey Map   Date :

Persona	User State	Journey (inc. tasks)	Channels	Content

stomer-Journey Map				Date :
sona	User State	Journey (inc. tasks)	Channels	Content

PROJECT NAME: _____   NOTE: _____

Customer-Journey Map				Date:
Persona	User State	Journey (inc. tasks)	Channels	Content

stomer-Journey Map				Date:
sona	User State	Journey (inc. tasks)	Channels	Content

Customer-Journey Map

Date :

Persona	User State	Journey (inc. tasks)	Channels	Content

stomer-Journey Map				Date :
sona	User State	Journey (inc. tasks)	Channels	Content

PROJECT NAME: _____   NOTE: _____

Customer-Journey Map				Date :
Persona	User State	Journey (inc. tasks)	Channels	Content

stomer-Journey Map				Date:
sona	User State	Journey (inc. tasks)	Channels	Content

PROJECT NAME: _____   NOTE: _____

Customer-Journey Map				Date:
Persona	User State	Journey (inc. tasks)	Channels	Content

stomer-Journey Map				Date:
sona	User State	Journey (inc. tasks)	Channels	Content

Customer-Journey Map

Date :

Persona	User State	Journey (inc. tasks)	Channels	Content

stomer-Journey Map				Date :
˙sona	User State	Journey (inc. tasks)	Channels	Content

PROJECT NAME: _____   NOTE: _____

Customer-Journey Map   Date :

Persona	User State	Journey (inc. tasks)	Channels	Content

sona	User State	Journey (inc. tasks)	Channels	Content

stomer-Journey Map   Date:

Customer-Journey Map

Date :

Persona	User State	Journey (inc. tasks)	Channels	Content

slomer-Journey Map				Date :
sona	User State	Journey (inc. tasks)	Channels	Content

PROJECT NAME: _____   NOTE: _____

Customer-Journey Map				Date:
Persona	User State	Journey (inc. tasks)	Channels	Content

stomer-Journey Map				Date :
sona	User State	Journey (inc. tasks)	Channels	Content

Customer-Journey Map   Date :

Persona	User State	Journey (inc. tasks)	Channels	Content

sona	User State	Journey (inc. tasks)	Channels	Content

stomer-Journey Map   Date :

Customer-Journey Map				Date :
Persona	User State	Journey (inc. tasks)	Channels	Content

stomer-Journey Map				Date :
sona	User State	Journey (inc. tasks)	Channels	Content

PROJECT NAME: _____   NOTE: _____

Customer-Journey Map				Date:
Persona	User State	Journey (inc. tasks)	Channels	Content

stomer-Journey Map				Date :
sona	User State	Journey (inc. tasks)	Channels	Content

PROJECT NAME: _____   NOTE: _____

Customer-Journey Map				Date:
Persona	User State	Journey (inc. tasks)	Channels	Content

sɭomer-Journey Map				Date :
ʳsona	User State	Journey (inc. tasks)	Channels	Content

PROJECT NAME: _____   NOTE: _____

Customer-Journey Map   Date:

Persona	User State	Journey (inc. tasks)	Channels	Content

stomer-Journey Map				Date :
sona	User State	Journey (inc. tasks)	Channels	Content

PROJECT NAME: _____   NOTE: _____

Customer-Journey Map				Date :
Persona	User State	Journey (inc. tasks)	Channels	Content

stomer-Journey Map				Date :
sona	User State	Journey (inc. tasks)	Channels	Content

PROJECT NAME: _____   NOTE: _____

Customer-Journey Map				Date :
Persona	User State	Journey (inc. tasks)	Channels	Content

stomer-Journey Map				Date :
sona	User State	Journey (inc. tasks)	Channels	Content

Customer-Journey Map

Date :

Persona	User State	Journey (inc. tasks)	Channels	Content

stomer-Journey Map				Date :
sona	User State	Journey (inc. tasks)	Channels	Content

Customer-Journey Map				Date:
Persona	User State	Journey (inc. tasks)	Channels	Content

stomer-Journey Map   Date :

sona	User State	Journey (inc. tasks)	Channels	Content

PROJECT NAME: _____   NOTE: _____

Customer-Journey Map				Date:
Persona	User State	Journey (inc. tasks)	Channels	Content

stomer-Journey Map

Date:

sona	User State	Journey (inc. tasks)	Channels	Content

PROJECT NAME: _____   NOTE: _____

Customer-Journey Map				Date:
Persona	User State	Journey (inc. tasks)	Channels	Content

stomer-Journey Map   Date :

sona	User State	Journey (inc. tasks)	Channels	Content

Customer-Journey Map

Date:

Persona	User State	Journey (inc. tasks)	Channels	Content

ECT NAME: _____   NOTE: _____

stomer-Journey Map				Date:
sona	User State	Journey (inc. tasks)	Channels	Content

PROJECT NAME: _____   NOTE: _____

Customer-Journey Map				Date :
Persona	User State	Journey (inc. tasks)	Channels	Content

ECT NAME: _____   NOTE: _____

stomer-Journey Map				Date:
sona	User State	Journey (inc. tasks)	Channels	Content

PROJECT NAME: _____   NOTE: _____

Customer-Journey Map				Date:
Persona	User State	Journey (inc. tasks)	Channels	Content

ECT NAME: _____   NOTE: _____

slomer-Journey Map				Date:
sona	User State	Journey (inc. tasks)	Channels	Content

Customer-Journey Map   Date :

Persona	User State	Journey (inc. tasks)	Channels	Content

stomer-Journey Map				Date :
sona	User State	Journey (inc. tasks)	Channels	Content

PROJECT NAME: _____   NOTE: _____

Customer-Journey Map				Date :
Persona	User State	Journey (inc. tasks)	Channels	Content

slomer-Journey Map				Date :
sona	User State	Journey (inc. tasks)	Channels	Content

Customer-Journey Map

Date :

Persona	User State	Journey (inc. tasks)	Channels	Content

stomer-Journey Map				Date :
sona	User State	Journey (inc. tasks)	Channels	Content

Customer-Journey Map

Date:

Persona	User State	Journey (inc. tasks)	Channels	Content

stomer-Journey Map				Date :
sona	User State	Journey (inc. tasks)	Channels	Content

Customer-Journey Map

Date:

Persona	User State	Journey (inc. tasks)	Channels	Content

stomer-Journey Map				Date :
sona	User State	Journey (inc. tasks)	Channels	Content

PROJECT NAME: _____   NOTE: _____

Customer-Journey Map				Date :
Persona	User State	Journey (inc. tasks)	Channels	Content

stomer-Journey Map				Date:
sona	User State	Journey (inc. tasks)	Channels	Content

PROJECT NAME: _____   NOTE: _____

Customer-Journey Map   Date:

Persona	User State	Journey (inc. tasks)	Channels	Content

sona	User State	Journey (inc. tasks)	Channels	Content

stomer-Journey Map   Date:

PROJECT NAME: _____   NOTE: _____

Customer-Journey Map				Date:
Persona	User State	Journey (inc. tasks)	Channels	Content

stomer-Journey Map				Date :
sona	User State	Journey (inc. tasks)	Channels	Content

PROJECT NAME: _____   NOTE: _____

Customer-Journey Map				Date:
Persona	User State	Journey (inc. tasks)	Channels	Content

ECT NAME: _____   NOTE: _____

stomer-Journey Map				Date :
sona	User State	Journey (inc. tasks)	Channels	Content

PROJECT NAME: _____   NOTE: _____

Customer-Journey Map				Date:
Persona	User State	Journey (inc. tasks)	Channels	Content

slomer-Journey Map				Date :
sona	User State	Journey (inc. tasks)	Channels	Content

PROJECT NAME: _____   NOTE: _____

Customer-Journey Map				Date:
Persona	User State	Journey (inc. tasks)	Channels	Content

sona	User State	Journey (inc. tasks)	Channels	Content

stomer-Journey Map — Date:

PROJECT NAME: _____   NOTE: _____

Customer-Journey Map				Date:
Persona	User State	Journey (inc. tasks)	Channels	Content

stomer-Journey Map				Date :
sona	User State	Journey (inc. tasks)	Channels	Content

PROJECT NAME: _____   NOTE: _____

Customer-Journey Map				Date:
Persona	User State	Journey (inc. tasks)	Channels	Content

stomer-Journey Map				Date:
sona	User State	Journey (inc. tasks)	Channels	Content

PROJECT NAME: _____   NOTE: _____

Customer-Journey Map				Date:
Persona	User State	Journey (inc. tasks)	Channels	Content

stomer-Journey Map				Date :
sona	User State	Journey (inc. tasks)	Channels	Content

PROJECT NAME: _____   NOTE: _____

Customer-Journey Map				Date:
Persona	User State	Journey (inc. tasks)	Channels	Content

stomer-Journey Map   Date :

sona	User State	Journey (inc. tasks)	Channels	Content

PROJECT NAME: _____   NOTE: _____

Customer-Journey Map				Date:
Persona	User State	Journey (inc. tasks)	Channels	Content

stomer-Journey Map   Date :

sona	User State	Journey (inc. tasks)	Channels	Content

Customer-Journey Map

Date:

Persona	User State	Journey (inc. tasks)	Channels	Content

stomer-Journey Map   Date :

sona	User State	Journey (inc. tasks)	Channels	Content

Customer-Journey Map				Date:
Persona	User State	Journey (inc. tasks)	Channels	Content

stomer-Journey Map				Date :
sona	User State	Journey (inc. tasks)	Channels	Content

PROJECT NAME: _____   NOTE: _____

Customer-Journey Map				Date:
Persona	User State	Journey (inc. tasks)	Channels	Content

ECT NAME: _____   NOTE: _____

sona	User State	Journey (inc. tasks)	Channels	Content

stomer-Journey Map   Date :

PROJECT NAME: _____   NOTE: _____

Customer-Journey Map				Date:
Persona	User State	Journey (inc. tasks)	Channels	Content

stomer-Journey Map				Date:
sona	User State	Journey (inc. tasks)	Channels	Content

PROJECT NAME: _____   NOTE: _____

Customer-Journey Map				Date:
Persona	User State	Journey (inc. tasks)	Channels	Content

slomer-Journey Map				Date:
sona	User State	Journey (inc. tasks)	Channels	Content

Customer-Journey Map

Date :

Persona	User State	Journey (inc. tasks)	Channels	Content

stomer-Journey Map				Date:
sona	User State	Journey (inc. tasks)	Channels	Content

Customer-Journey Map

Date:

Persona	User State	Journey (inc. tasks)	Channels	Content

stomer-Journey Map				Date:
sona	User State	Journey (inc. tasks)	Channels	Content

Customer-Journey Map

Date:

Persona	User State	Journey (inc. tasks)	Channels	Content

stomer-Journey Map				Date:
sona	User State	Journey (inc. tasks)	Channels	Content

PROJECT NAME: _____   NOTE: _____

Customer-Journey Map				Date:
Persona	User State	Journey (inc. tasks)	Channels	Content

ECT NAME: _____   NOTE: _____

slomer-Journey Map				Date :
sona	User State	Journey (inc. tasks)	Channels	Content

PROJECT NAME: _____ NOTE: _____

Customer-Journey Map				Date:
Persona	User State	Journey (inc. tasks)	Channels	Content

stomer-Journey Map

Date :

sona	User State	Journey (inc. tasks)	Channels	Content

Takeaway notes:

_____

_____

_____

_____

_____

Year of use:

_____

Made in United States
Troutdale, OR
02/13/2025

28975463R00071